Seven Days in a Week

By Catherine Ripley

CELEBRATION PRESS
Pearson Learning Group

Long ago people used calendars.

Mexican calendar from long ago

People today use calendars, too.

JANUARY

Sunday	Monday	Tuesday	Wednesday	Thursday	Friday	Saturday
1	2	3	4	5	6	7
8	9	10	11	12	13	14
15	16	17	18	19	20	21
22	23	24	25	26	27	28
29	30	31				

Calendars show the months of the year. They also show the days of the week.

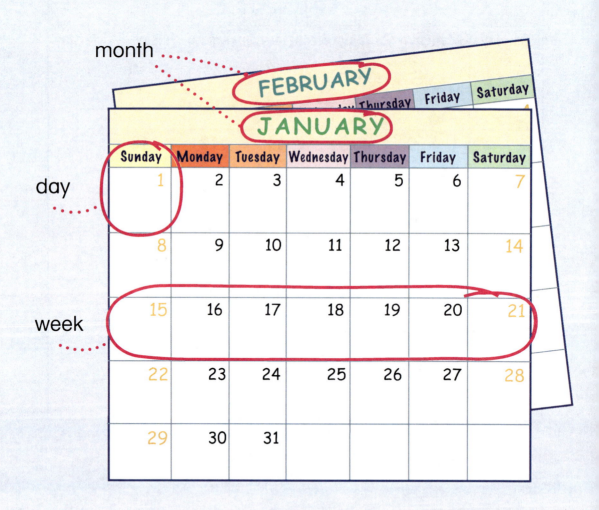

4

The days of the week are Sunday, Monday, Tuesday, Wednesday, Thursday, Friday, and Saturday.

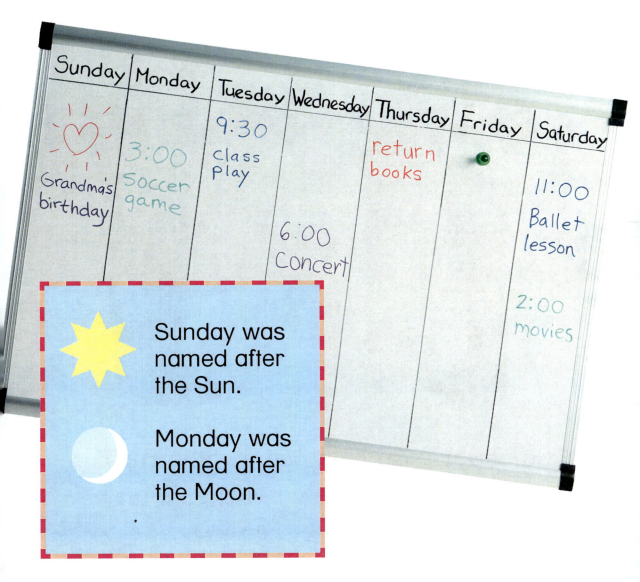

Sunday was named after the Sun.

Monday was named after the Moon.

Calendars can help people plan their week. They can see what they plan to do on each day of the week.

A class can use a calendar. It helps the children know what they will do each day of the week.

Calendars help us plan our days.